CHESS STRATEGY FOR BEGINNERS

Chess
Strategy

FOR BEGINNERS

Winning Maneuvers
to Master the Game

Jessica Era Martin

Illustrations by Collaborate Agency

callisto
publishing
an imprint of Sourcebooks

Copyright © 2022 by Callisto Publishing LLC
Cover and internal design © 2022 by Callisto Publishing LLC
Illustrations © 2022 Collaborate Agency
Author photograph courtesy of Molly Wilbanks
Interior and Cover Designer: Jennifer Hsu
Art Producer: Megan Baggott
Editor: Van Van Cleave
Production Editor: Matthew Burnett
Production Manager: Martin Worthington

Published by Callisto Publishing LLC C/O Sourcebooks LLC

P.O. Box 4410, Naperville, Illinois 60567-4410
(630) 961-3900
callistopublishing.com

Printed in the United States of America
VP 9

This book is dedicated to my son Albert,
whose inquisitiveness and compassion
remind me to pay attention.

Contents

Introduction

Whenever I want to impress someone, I say, "I'm a chess teacher," or, "I'm passionate about studying chess—I've been hooked since I was five." That this sounds impressive speaks to a cultural belief that chess players are inherently smart, and smartness is something that is valued. But I'm going to posit that chess players are not necessarily inherently intelligent. Anyone can play chess and improve their game. Chess has real-life applications, and as you improve your chess, you will also sharpen your skills of concentration, visualization, risk/benefit analysis, critical thinking, and problem-solving—as well as increase your patience (both with yourself and others).

This book will first provide an overview of the basics of the game, including the board layout, the rules, and the roles of the various pieces, then examine 30 of the most effective strategies for beginner- to intermediate-level chess players. Test your memory and understanding via the Challenges chapter at the end, which includes an answer key.

While there are thousands of patterns in chess, the more you practice, the more often you will recognize strategic and tactical patterns in your own games.

It is my hope that this book will encourage your love of chess. It's a game that can be played at any age and anywhere in the world. It's known as the great equalizer because it is universal: Your background doesn't matter to chess. And, of course, chess is fun!

PART I

Chess Basics

The earliest precursor to chess, as we know it today, was in India around 600 CE. The International Chess Federation (FIDE) has estimated that 605 million people play chess, and according to *The Boston Globe*, Chess.com onboarded about 11.1 million *new* users from March to November of 2020. In 2020, the polling organization YouGov found that 70 percent of adults around the world have played chess at some point in their lives.

The first two chapters of this book will cover the goals, rules, and notation of chess, which will be essential to understanding the following chapters and being able to read the diagrams throughout the book. Let's dive in!

CHAPTER ONE

The Fundamentals of Chess

GET IN A STRATEGIC MINDSET

It's true that everyone can learn specific strategies to become a better chess player, but it's also important to make sure you are prepared for the game psychologically. Let's look at five characteristics you should try to channel while playing chess.

Patience: Improvement doesn't happen overnight, so be patient with yourself.

Compassion: Everyone makes mistakes and finds certain parts of the game challenging. Be kind to yourself as you focus on the process, not the product.

Curiosity: There is always more to learn! Take any position you have questions about, and set it up on your own board. Maneuver the pieces to be sure you completely understand it. Plug it into an analysis program on a website like Chess.com or Lichess.org to see all the possibilities.

Open-mindedness: It might not be immediately clear why a certain strategy is recommended by a chess coach or engine. Or maybe you have a preconceived notion that something else works better. Try it out! Create your own statistics to see what really works best for you.

Focus: As with learning a new language or musical instrument, you must prioritize and commit to practicing chess in order to improve.

THE BOARD

The chessboard is a perfect eight-by-eight grid, composed of thirty-two white and thirty-two black squares. The rows of the board are called ranks (a through h), and the columns are called files (1 through 8). In the starting position, each player's set of pieces faces the other's, sitting on the two ranks closest to each player. Later, you will also learn about the queenside (the half of the board where a player's queen starts) and the kingside (the half where the king starts).

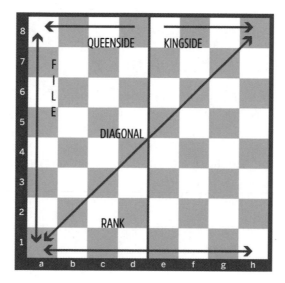

CHESS LINGO

Before diving into the specifics of the board and pieces, let's start with some basic chess terminology.

Active/Passive: A piece is considered active when it controls squares and is involved in the attack. A passive piece is one that is stuck defending and cannot participate in the attack.

Check: Check occurs when a piece attacks the king, but the king can move, you can block the check, or you can capture the checking piece to escape from danger. You must do one of these three things to get out of check.

Checkmate: This is how you win the game. Checkmate (sometimes called "mate") occurs when the king is in check and there is no safe way to move, block, or capture to escape from the check. When you make a checkmate, the game ends. You can bow or shake hands and say, "Good game!"

Legal/Illegal: A move is legal if it follows how a piece is allowed to move or capture. Note that it is illegal to capture a king in chess; therefore, it is against the rules to put your own king into danger. See pages 8–14 for how pieces move.

Material: This refers to the chess pieces.

Strategy: Strategy refers to a longer-term plan to improve your position.

Tactics: These are short-term tricks to quickly help you win material or create a checkmate. See pages 28–31 for examples.

Tempo: Referring to time, if you accomplish two goals with one move, you "gain a tempo," and if you move a piece twice in the opening or otherwise waste time, you "lose a tempo."

THE PIECES

In a chess game, a player controls either the black or white pieces, and each piece is useful in its own way. The pieces are generally assigned a numerical value to help decide which exchanges are beneficial to which player and to guide strategy. ("Points" are not tallied or kept at the end of the game; checkmate always wins!) Note that you take turns in chess, there is no "passing," and you can capture only one piece at a time.

Pawn

Number per player: 8 • **Relative value:** 1 point each

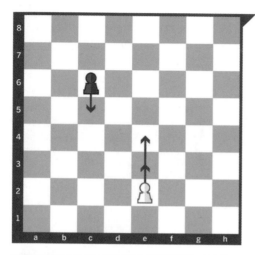

Movement: Pawns always move forward. On their first move, they may advance one or two squares forward. After that, they may only move one square at a time. If they reach the other side of the board, they can promote into a different piece (see page 9).

Captures: Pawns capture diagonally one square forward. They are the only pieces that capture differently from how they move. A special variation of their diagonal capture is called "en passant" (see page 9).

Role in strategy: Pawns create the structure that determines where your pieces will go. Additionally, pawn moves are committal because they never go backward!

EN PASSANT

This French term means "in passing." If an opponent's pawn advances past your pawn's regular diagonal capture square so that it sits directly next to yours, you can still take it using this special rule. To determine if you can capture en passant, ask yourself if your pawn and your opponent's pawn are side by side and if their pawn moved two squares immediately prior to your move. If yes to both, you may capture by moving diagonally forward and simply removing the adjacent pawn! The pawn will disappear automatically if you make this capture online. If you want to capture en passant, you must do so on the turn immediately following your opponent's pawn move or you will lose the opportunity.

PROMOTION

When a pawn reaches the other side of the board, it can promote, which means it can turn into your choice of a queen, rook, bishop, or knight. It cannot become another king and cannot remain a pawn. Most of the time, you'll promote into a queen because it is the most powerful piece. Promotion generally occurs in the endgame. On some rare occasions, you may want to "underpromote" your pawn, or turn it into a rook, bishop, or knight. This can be a useful move if you need to avoid a stalemate (more on that later).

Knight

Number per player: 2 • **Relative value:** 3 points each

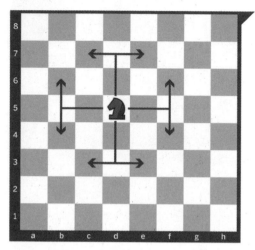

Movement: The knight moves in an "L" shape, two squares in one direction and one more square in a perpendicular direction. The "L" shape can face any direction, including backward (upside-down or sideways "L"s are also okay). Additionally, the knight is the only piece that can jump over other pieces, both black and white.

Captures: Knights capture the piece they land on at the end of their jump. They do not capture anything along the way.

Role in strategy: Knights are sneaky and great at attacking two pieces at once, known as a fork (page 28).

Bishop

Number per player: 2 • **Relative value:** 3 points each

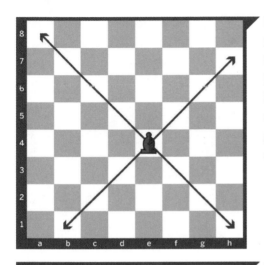

Movement: The bishop can move any number of squares it wants diagonally. Each bishop stays on the color of its starting square; bishops on different colors are distinguished as "dark-squared" or "light-squared."

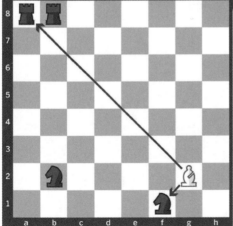

Captures: Same as movement.

Role in strategy: Bishops are excellent at attacking from a distance. They're also great at creating pins (see page 28), and later they are useful for supporting queens in batteries to threaten checkmate. Developing a bishop to the longest diagonal of the board is called a "fianchetto" (pronounced "fee-an-ketto"). It is a strong way to attack the center as well as the opposite corner of the board.

Rook

Number per player: 2 • **Relative value:** 5 points each

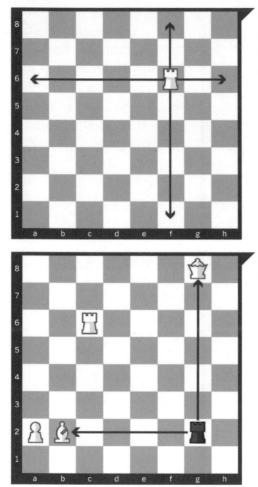

Movement: The rook moves along files and ranks as far as it wants, forward or backward.

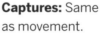

Captures: Same as movement.

Role in strategy: Rooks usually become active in the middle game once there are open files. The rook is a great attacking piece, especially when it works with a queen or another rook. Rooks are good for doubling up, creating pins, and attacking the seventh rank. It's also helpful to leave a rook near the king after castling, for protection. In the endgame, rooks can help protect a pawn as it travels up the board to promote.

Queen

Number per player: 1 • **Relative value:** 9 points

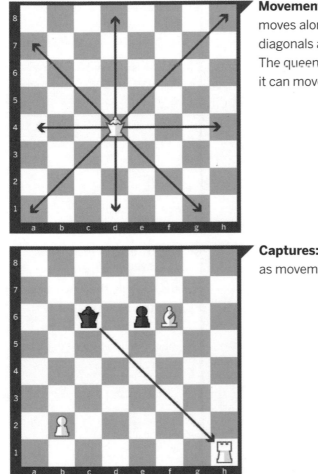

Movement: The queen moves along files, ranks, and diagonals as far as it wants. The queen doesn't jump but it can move backward.

Captures: Same as movement.

Role in strategy: The queen is great at attacking multiple pieces and, most important, at checkmating. It'd rather not hang back and protect pawns, but be careful not to develop it too early, or it'll get kicked by the other pieces.

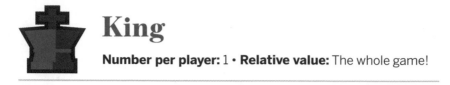

King

Number per player: 1 • **Relative value:** The whole game!

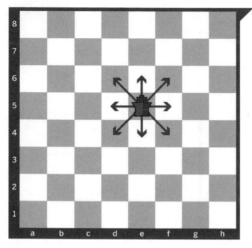

Movement: The king can move one square in any direction. However, the king can't legally move onto a square that puts it in danger.

Captures: Same as legal movement. In the game shown here, the king can capture the bishop, but it cannot capture the rook, because then it would still be in check by the bishop.

Role in strategy: Always protect your king! One way to do this is to castle (see page 15). In the endgame, when the queens have usually come off the board, the king becomes a fighting piece and can help attack pawns or shepherd a pawn to its promotion square.

CASTLING

Castling is a unique move that helps you protect your king by getting it out of the center of the board. When castling, the king goes two squares toward either rook (kingside or queenside), and, in the same turn, the rook jumps over the king and lands right next to it. You may only castle if the five following conditions are met:

→ There are no pieces between your king and rook

→ Your king and rook have not yet moved

→ You are not currently in check

→ You do not land in check

→ You do not "go through" check (the king travels two squares to castle, and you may not be in check at any point along that path)

You can only castle once in a game. It's usually best to try to do so as soon as possible.

GAME PLAY

In chess, white always moves first, but this does not in any way mean white always wins. In tournaments, a computer will decide the pairings and who gets which color, alternating every round. In casual play, you can hide a white pawn in one hand and a black pawn in the other and ask your opponent to choose one of your hands. Whichever color is in that hand is the color that they will play with.

When setting up your board, make sure that a white square is in the right-hand corner closest to you. If you have letters and numbers on your board, the first and second ranks are for the white pieces and the seventh and eighth are for black. The queens always sit on their corresponding colors.

Game play has three different stages: the opening, the middle game, and the endgame. Later, we'll discuss specific strategies for each stage.

Opening

This is the beginning of the game! The focus is on getting your pieces into strong positions to prepare for the action of the middle game. There are many reasonable ways to get your pieces and pawns out, but the most important thing is to ensure your king's safety. I suggest castling within the first 10 moves (the fastest path to castling only takes 4 moves!). Once you're castled, the opening is generally considered completed.

Middle Game

This is where the action is! Both players typically have castled and are now planning an attack on the kingside, queenside, or center of the board. Players will be capturing hanging (unprotected) pieces, looking for tactics, aiming for the king, and coordinating pieces to work toward checkmates. For this reason, many games are decided in the middle game.

Endgame

The position is generally considered to be an endgame when most of the pieces, especially the queens, are off the board. The goal of the endgame is typically to promote a pawn, as it is much easier to checkmate your opponent with a queen or additional material on the board (although it's not required).

Many chess games end in checkmate, as shown in the diagram at right.

Black has white in checkmate! The white king cannot move, nothing can block check from the black queen, and the king cannot capture the queen because it is guarded by a pawn. A player may never put their own king in check.

However, some games end in what's called a draw instead—a tie between players, often irrespective of who has more points or pieces at the time of the draw. Draws, like checkmates, can occur at any stage of the game but happen most commonly in the middle or endgame. A draw can occur in the following ways:

1. **Agreement:** You can offer a draw or accept a draw offer if you feel you are in an equal or slightly worse position compared to your opponent.

2. **Stalemate:** This occurs when a player's king is not in check but they have no legal moves (with the king or any other pieces). In the diagram below, it is black's move, and it is therefore stalemate.

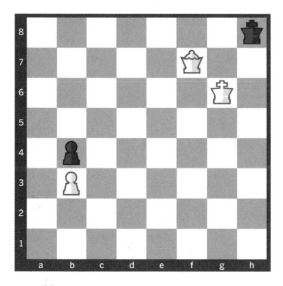

3. **Threefold Repetition:** To prevent players from repeating a position endlessly, there is a rule in chess whereby a game ends in a draw if the same position (the exact same configuration of pieces) appears on the board three times. The same moves leading into the position do not have to be made in the same order, but the same position does have to occur three distinct times.

4. **Fifty-Move Rule:** This rule prevents a game from going on forever. If you don't know the technique for checkmating with certain pieces

and just dance around the board for fifty moves without moving a pawn or capturing a piece, the game ends in a draw. Note that a complete move includes both white's and black's turn.

5. **Insufficient Mating Material:** This rule can be claimed when there are not enough pieces left on the board to make a checkmate happen! For example, if both sides have only a king remaining, that's an automatic draw.

Remember, a draw is better than a loss, so don't give up, even in a bad position!

UNDERSTANDING NOTATION

Recording an entire chess game may sound daunting, but there is a system called algebraic notation that makes it easy. Algebraic notation even lets us replay historic games! Consider writing your moves down (online, it's done for you automatically) so you can review your games and analyze them for mistakes.

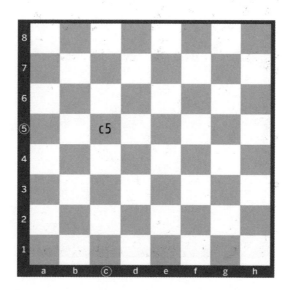

In algebraic notation, the pieces are referred to with the following letters:

King	K
Queen	Q
Rook	R
Bishop	B
Knight	N
Pawn	(blank; no capital letter at all)

To record a move, write down the move number and the letter of the piece that moved, followed by the coordinates of the square that it landed on. For example: "1. Nf3" means a knight moved to the square f3 on the first move. If two coordinates follow a move number (ex. 1. e4 e5) that means that on the first move, white moves a pawn to e4 and black moves a pawn to e5.

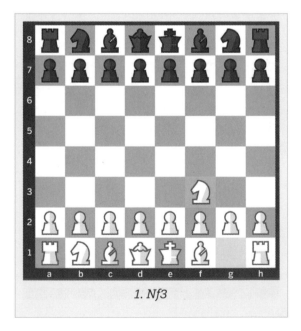

1. Nf3

If two of the same kind of piece could have moved to the same square, indicate the starting position, either the file or the rank (whichever can differentiate between the pieces), of the piece that moved.

In this game, Grandmaster (GM) Shakhriyar Mamedyarov played 12. Rfe1 next.

When a move results in a capture, check, or checkmate, special notations are added. Castling uses different notation as well. Here are the specific symbols used in each instance:

A piece that is not a pawn makes a capture	x (between the capturing piece and the square it lands on—e.g., "Bxf6")
A pawn makes a capture	x (between the file the pawn starts on and the square it lands on—e.g., "cxd4." If a pawn captures another pawn, you can also just write the files the pawn starts and lands on—e.g., "cd")
Check	+ (after the notation—e.g., "Re1+")
Checkmate	# (after the notation—e.g., "Qf7#")

Castles kingside	0-0
Castles queenside	0-0-0
Promotion	=
Black's move when white's move is not listed	. . .

You may notice a question mark or exclamation mark after certain moves in this book. These annotations are added while conducting postgame analysis to indicate a good move (!) or a bad move (?). There are other annotations, but these are the most common. Note that it's against tournament rules to annotate during a game.

Yip plays 35 . . . gxf3 and International Master (IM) Nazi Paikidze resigns. IM Carissa Yip is the 2021 U.S. Women's Chess Champion at eighteen years old!

GM Wesley So plays 10. de (dxe5 is also acceptable notation). So is a three-time U.S. Chess Champion.

CHAPTER TWO

General Principles and Tactics

SIX BASIC PRINCIPLES FOR BEGINNERS

At every stage of the game, there are certain goals you should strive to accomplish. Read on to learn about six foundational principles of chess.

1. Control Space in the Center of the Board

In the opening, you want to occupy or control the most critical part of the board: the center: e4, d4, e5, and d5. Aim your pawns, knights, and bishops at the middle. Consider how a knight on the edge of the board in the opening can only move to two new squares, whereas in the center it can move to four. That's twice as many options for attack!

2. Develop, Activate, and Harmonize Your Pieces

It's important to get your pieces involved in the game. If you aren't sure what to do, ask yourself if any of your pieces can get to better squares where they have more freedom of movement and are poised to attack.

Pieces love to work together. Rooks are twice as powerful doubled, queens and bishops make great batteries when they are lined up together, and queens and knights complement each other in mating attacks.

3. Castle Early

You should be ready to castle in the first 4 to 10 moves of the game. Because all the action is happening in the center, you do *not* want your king there! Castling helps protect it. If your opponent leaves their king in the center for too long, open up the middle with pawn trades and attack quickly.

4. Look for Hanging Pieces

A hanging piece is one that is unprotected or worth more than the piece used to capture it. It can therefore be captured for free or at minimal cost. Remember that different kinds of pieces have different values (see pages 8–14). Naturally, you will want to capture pieces for free when possible. When deciding if you should capture a piece in a situation where you'll be captured back, figure out who will get more points from the exchange. For example, it's worth taking a knight (three points) with a pawn (one point), even if you'll lose that pawn. In that exchange, you'll earn two points. (We don't keep track of points after the game is over, but whoever is ahead in material during the game often has a better position.)

5. Ask "What's the Threat?" After Your Opponent's Move

Before you move, ask yourself why your opponent made their last move. Are they attacking something? If their threat is nothing to be concerned about or your threats are faster, continue with your plan. But if their threat is dangerous, you must react.

6. Consider Your Pawn Structure

Pawns can guard squares and each other. They do not like to be left behind ("backward"), "doubled," or "isolated." Don't play checkers if you're playing chess; if all your pawns are on white squares, your dark squares become weak. Every pawn move creates a weakness! Don't move too many pawns early on, or you might not have time to develop your pieces; and don't move too many pawns in front of your castled king, or it will be wide open for an attack.

SIX TACTICS TO KNOW

Before diving into strategies, let's look at six common tactics to help you win material and checkmate your opponent.

1. Fork/Double Attack

A fork occurs when one piece attacks two. Make sure to attack pieces that are either hanging or more valuable than the attacking piece, and that you can't be attacked back. A double attack occurs when one piece aims at two things—for example, a hanging piece and a checkmate. The

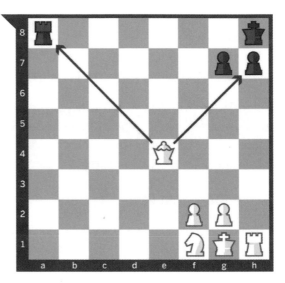

best thing about forks and double attacks is that although your opponent can move one piece out of the way, you'll still get the other piece or square.

2. Pin

A pin involves three pieces in a straight line (a file, rank, or diagonal). Your attacking piece should be pointed at two of your opponent's pieces, one of which is shielded by the other. The piece in the middle can't or shouldn't move because it needs to block your attack from reaching the more valuable

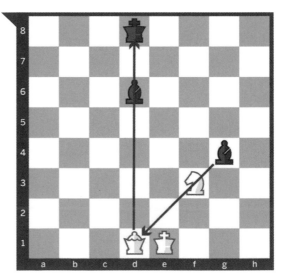

piece behind it. If the piece in the back is a king (and the middle piece therefore can't legally move), this is called an absolute pin. A relative pin is one in which the middle piece could move but doesn't want to because the piece behind it could then be captured. You can exploit a pin by capturing something the pinned piece no longer protects.

Sometimes you won't want to capture the pinned piece (for example, if it's worth fewer points than your attacking piece). In that case, you can put more pressure on the pinned piece instead. Pressure simply means attacking the pinned piece again with another piece. Since it can't move, you have time to bring another piece in. This way, you'll have more attackers on the pinned piece than your opponent has defenders, and you can win material.

3. Skewer

A skewer is another long-range attack. As in a pin, three pieces are lined up, but in a skewer, the piece in the middle is the more valuable one, not the one in the back. Once your opponent moves the middle piece to safety, you can win the piece behind it. Some call this tactic an "x-ray."

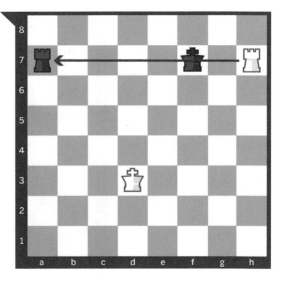

4. Discovered Attack/Check

Discoveries are also long-range attacks involving three pieces. However, this time, the piece in the middle is yours, not your opponent's. When you move the piece in the middle, you reveal an attack from your other piece against your opponent's piece. A discovered check occurs when the revealed attack is against your opponent's king. This tactic gives your middle piece the ability to move basically anywhere safely, since your opponent's following turn must be used to get out of check! The discovered double check, in which both the piece that moves and the piece behind it attack your opponent's king, is the most forcing move in chess.

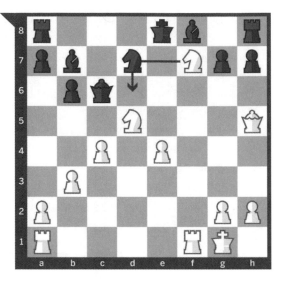

5. Remove the Guard

You want something, but it's being protected? Eliminate the piece that's guarding what you want. Then capture the newly hanging piece. In the diagram, after you capture the knight, h7 will be hanging. So if the pawn captures your rook back, you can play Qxh7#. If they play . . . g6 to stop the checkmate, you've just won a knight for free.

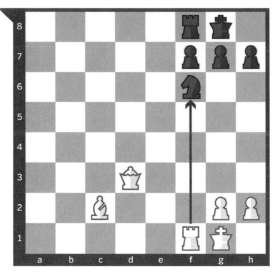

6. Decoy/Deflection

These tactics are similar in that they both lure a piece away from what it guards instead of directly capturing the guarding piece (removing the guard). This tactic involves a sacrifice of material.

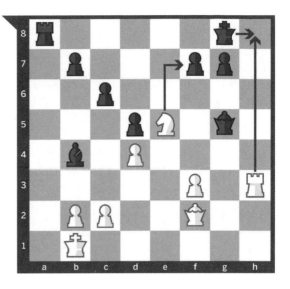

In this position, white can play Rh8+ to lure black's king away from the pawn on f7. It's not that white just wants a pawn, as a pawn is worth less than a rook. The point is that once black's king is on h8, Nxf7+ forks the king and the queen, and white wins material!

PART II

Strategies for Every Stage of the Game

Now that you know the rules and principles of chess, the next three chapters will go over specific strategies for the opening, middle game, and endgame, respectively. After you've mastered the strategies provided here, you can practice what you've learned in the Challenges chapter, which is followed by an answer key you can use to check your moves.

CHAPTER THREE

Opening Strategies

· ·

The following seven openings are specific lines, starting with novice material everyone needs to know (tricks and traps to use and to avoid) followed by top-level professional openings that you can play at any skill level. Understanding these seven strategies will prepare you with the confidence and theory you need to start a game on the right foot, whether you're playing as white or black.

SCHOLAR'S MATE

The first opening trick everyone needs to know is the Four-Move Mate (aka Scholar's Mate). The first move for white in this line is 1. e4. This allows your queen and bishop to develop, which makes for quick tactics. Notice the f7 square is only defended by black's king. It's a light square, and you've just opened up your long-range light-squared pieces.

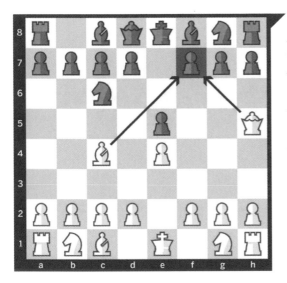

Black can play 1 . . . e5. And now, 2. Qh5. From here the queen does two things: it pins the pawn on f7, and it attacks the hanging pawn on e5. Black should guard the pawn on e5 with 2 . . . Nc6. Obviously, if the queen immediately takes on f7, it will just get captured. So, you add an attacker with 3. Bc4. Now there's a real threat!

Black should play 3 . . . g6 to block the queen or 3 . . . Qe7 to protect the pawn on f7 twice. If black plays the most natural-looking move, 3 . . . Nf6, which is super common at the beginner level, white can create the Scholar's Mate by swooping in on f7: 4. Qxf7#.

Oops! Game over. 3 . . . Nf6 didn't stop the checkmate on f7.

Black played 3 . . . g6, stopping checkmate—for now!

Tip for black: You can try the same trick on white by targeting the square f2.

GIUOCO PIANO, OR ITALIAN GAME

Giuoco Piano means "quiet game" in Italian, but this opening is anything but quiet! Most people refer to it simply as the Italian or the Italian Game. This opening is one of the quickest ways to castle and aims at the weakest square on black's side of the board, f7.

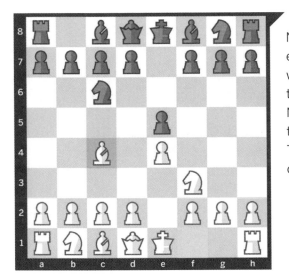

It begins with 1. e4 e5. Now 2. Nf3 attacks the e5 pawn. Black's best way of guarding it is with the knight: 2 . . . Nc6. Next, white brings out their bishop with 3. Bc4. This aims at both the center and f7.

If black plays 3 . . . Nf6, white has 4. Ng5, *also* aiming at f7! Then, Black has to play 4 . . . d5, or else white will play 5. Nxf7 and fork the queen and the rook. Note that the black king can't take the knight in this line because it is guarded by the bishop on c4.

The Italian is rife with tactical opportunities, and the first three moves for white—1. e4, 2. Nf3, 3. Bc4—can be played against a variety of black's maneuvers.

Tip for white: Attack f7 quickly and open the center with a pawn trade (c3 first, then d4).

Tips for black: It's best to prevent 4. Ng5 by playing 3 . . . Bc5. This attacks white's f2 pawn and leaves the queen open to defend g5. White can no longer play 4. Ng5 because the knight would be taken by the queen! Castle early and watch for tactics. Try to get in d5 when you can!

If 3 . . . Bc5 white can't play 4. Ng5 safely.

FRIED LIVER

Yes, that's really what it's called! The Fried Liver expands upon the Italian Game. After the first three moves of the Italian, if black plays 3 . . . Nf6, white has 4. Ng5, threatening to take on f7.

Black plays 4 . . . d5, the only way to stop the immediate capture of f7.

Now white takes on d5 with the pawn: 5. ed. And here's where it gets fun! Black's most natural-looking move, 5 . . . Nxd5, is no good. White can sacrifice and attack ("sac and attack") with 6. Nxf7! (a decoy).

Even though white's bishop isn't guarding the knight on f7, the sacrifice accomplishes something valuable: It brings the king out! After 6 . . . Kxf7, white has 7. Qf3+, a double attack on the knight and king. The black knight cannot move back to f6 to block the check and save itself because it is pinned to the king by the bishop on c4.

And if black plays the awful 7 . . . Kg8, it's mate along the diagonal, white takes on d5 with either the queen or the bishop. Black can take back on d5 with the queen, then block the check for a second with a bishop on e6, but white just takes on d5 and e6, and it's officially mate.

Better for black is 7 . . . Ke6, which holds on to the knight. However, the knight is still pinned, and white can put more pressure on it with 8. Nc3!

Tips for black: After 4. ed, you have to move your c6-knight. Try 4 . . . Na5 to attack the bishop on c4. Do not capture on d5 with your knight! Also, you can avoid the Fried Liver entirely by playing 3 . . . Bc5.

■ FRIED LIVER MOVES ■

1. e4	e5
2. Nf3	Nc6
3. Bc4 (Italian)	Nf6
4. Ng5	d5 (otherwise white plays Nxf7)
5. ed	If Nxd5, a common mistake (Na5 is better for black)
6. Nxf7	Kxf7
7. Qf3+	If Kg8
8. Bxd5+	Qxd5
9. Qxd5+	Be6
10. Qxe6#	
If 7 . . .	Ke6
8. Nc3	Nb4, guarding the knight again
9. 0-0 and play Re1, d4, etc. to attack the center!	

QUEEN'S GAMBIT

This is the oldest chess opening that is still played today! It was first mentioned in a manuscript in 1490 but didn't gain popularity until centuries later, when positional play was given more credence.

The Queen's Gambit presents another way to attack the center for white, starting with the queen's pawn: 1. d4. This discourages both 1 . . . e5 and 1 . . . c5 because white could just take those pawns. Black commonly responds 1 . . . d5 or 1 . . . Nf6. In either case, white plays 2. c4, which creates a pawn wall.

This opening is a gambit because white appears to offer black a free pawn: 1. d4. White's c-pawn looks like it's hanging, but if black takes it with 2 . . . dc, known as the Queen's Gambit Accepted, white is able to win it back quite easily with either 3. e3 or 3. e4, opening a discovered attack on c4 from the white bishop on f1—or with the immediate 3. Qa4+, which is a double attack on the black king and the pawn on c4.

White has pulled black's d-pawn away from the center while maintaining both of their own center pawns.

More common at higher levels are 2 . . . e6, the Queen's Gambit Declined, or 2 . . . c6, the Slav Defense. After black plays 2 . . . e6, white develops the knight behind the c-pawn with 3. Nc3. Black can play the most common move, 3 . . . Nf6, to attack the center and prepare to castle. Notice that both players are maintaining tension in the center by not exchanging pawns.

White has many options to continue development. A common one, 4. Nf3, also known as the Queen's Gambit Declined: Three Knights Variation, looks like this.

Next, white will play moves like e3, Qc2, Bd3, and 0-0.

Most 1. d4 openings are considered strategic and positional, whereas 1. e4 is mainly tactical. Play both to get a feel for your preferred style, then focus on one and learn a variation that works for you!

Tip for white: In any queen's pawn opening, it's important to bring your c-pawn out before developing the knight to c3. Otherwise, your position will be cramped.

Tip for black: You can capture on c4 after white has played Bd3. Then white must spend another turn, or tempo, moving their bishop to capture back.

RUY LÓPEZ

This is another opening that's been studied for hundreds of years! It was introduced in 1561 but not popularized until the 1800s. It's a very theoretical opening but popular at all levels.

The first two moves are the same as most e4 openings—1. e4 e5 2. Nf3 Nc6—but now instead of the Italian with 3. Bc4, white plays 3. Bb5 to attack black's knight, which is guarding e5.

White does not take the knight right away, even though it looks like a good "remove the guard" tactic. This is because black can capture the bishop back with the d-pawn, and after white takes on e5 with the knight, black can play Qd4, forking the white knight on e5 and the pawn on e4 and consequently winning the pawn back. It's not worth giving up a bishop for a knight for this! (See pages 10 and 11 for more on the relative strengths of bishops and knights.)

1. e4	e5
2. Nf3	Nc6
3. Bb5	a6
If 4. Bxc6	dxc6
5. Nxe5	Qd4, forking
If 4. Ba4	Nf6

On move five after 4. Ba4 Nf6, white can castle.

With black, some players will kick the white bishop back again with 4 . . . b5 and some will play 4 . . . Nf6. There are lots of tricks in this opening. It can be a bit tough for black to find compensation for white's quick attack and control of the center, so it's also been called the Spanish Torture.

NIMZO-INDIAN DEFENSE

This opening for black is a solid way to respond to 1. d4. Black plays 1 . . . Nf6. Since black has not put a pawn in the center, white immediately creates a wall with 2. c4. Then, black brings out a center pawn with 2 . . . e6.

Next, white brings out a knight with 3. Nc3, and black attacks and pins it to the king with 3 . . . Bb4; this move defines the opening. Now black can castle on move 4 and capture the knight on c3 at some point, although it's not common to do so unless the bishop is challenged by a pawn push to a3.

White has many options on their fourth move. In general, they will have a stronger center than black. However, black's pin can be annoying, and by castling quickly, black is ready to attack. The Nimzo-Indian is a positionally sound defense that many players of all skill levels enjoy. The diagram to the left is an example of the middle game GM Aron Nimzowitsch played in 1926, following his eponymous opening.

Notice black traded the bishop for the knight on c3, doubling white's pawns on the c-file.

Tips for white: If you don't want to have your pawns doubled on the c-file, you can play 4. Qc2 and capture back with your queen in the event of an exchange on c3. If you don't mind the doubled pawns, continue to develop as normal, and try to open the position, as you'll have two bishops, and black will only have one after exchanging on c3.

Tip for black: If you trade the bishop for the knight, be sure to keep the position closed (no pawn trades) to benefit your two knights.

SICILIAN DEFENSE

The Sicilian is the most aggressive, tactical opening for black. It avoids countless opening traps that can happen when white plays 1. e4 and black responds with 1 . . . e5. Instead, black responds with the hypermodern 1 . . . c5, which attacks the center from the side. There are hundreds of variations of the Sicilian Defense. Here, you will learn the main ideas behind c5 and how black can best get their pieces developed and castle.

The open Sicilians are called such because at some point white plays d4 and the center opens up. Usually, white brings a knight to f3 to guard d4 first. Whenever white plays d4, black takes with the pawn on c5. Black thereby captures a center pawn with a flank pawn, meaning black still has both of their center pawns while white has only the e-pawn.

3 . . . cd! This common position occurs after:

1. e4 c5

2. Nf3 d6 (pawn chain!)

3. d4 cd

Now both sides commonly continue to develop with 4. Nxd4 and 4 . . . Nf6, which attacks e4. After white plays 5. Nc3 to guard e4, black has choices! Try 5 . . . a6 (the Najdorf), which prevents three pieces from annoying you on b5.

Or try 5 . . . g6 (the Dragon) to fianchetto the dark-squared bishop on the long diagonal.

White may opt to castle queenside, while black castles kingside. When opponents castle on opposite sides, whoever is the faster attacker usually wins.

CHAPTER FOUR

Middle Game Strategies

• •

The middle game is often when games are decided. This is because you must set yourself up in a good position to create tactics that can serve as a winning blow. When making a plan in the middle game, consider the following twelve strategies. As a reminder, always keep your guiding principles in mind:

1. Control space in the center of the board

2. Develop, activate, and harmonize your pieces

3. Castle early

4. Look for hanging pieces

5. Ask "What's the threat?" after your opponent's move

6. Consider your pawn structure

BUILD A PAWN CHAIN

Whenever you push a pawn forward, it creates space for your pieces to gain scope. However, every pawn push is committal; because pawns never go backward, they can't protect the squares they previously held, creating potential attacking points for your opponent.

The best way to guard your pawns is to build a "pawn chain," placing three pawns in a diagonal line. When your pawn chain points to the king- or queenside, it is called a "river of pawns," and you can line up attacking pieces to follow the river's direction. In this example, IM Carissa Yip captures with . . . gxf4 to extend her pawn chain. Notice her bishop and queen battery is also pointed at the king.

UNLEASH A PAWN STORM

Another pawn-related strategy you should know is the pawn storm. This is when you simply throw all your pawns at the opponent's king!

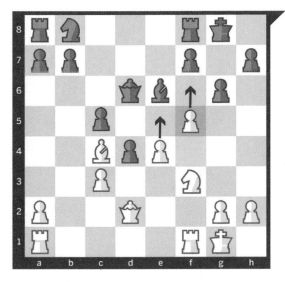

GM Viswanathan Anand demonstrates this against GM Ian Nepomniachtchi in the game on page 89 from the FIDE Chess.com Online Nations Cup in 2020. Anand plays 15. f5 and follows with e5 and f6, leaving his bishop and rook to get captured.

Notice because black has moved his g-pawn, there are two weaknesses around the king: f6 and h6.

Anand simply brings the queen in to h6, and there is no stopping Qg7# next! This is the power of a good pawn storm.

What not to do: Do not storm with the pawns in front of your castled king!

MAKE LUFT

Sometimes, when your king still has three pawns in front of it, your opponent will threaten a back-rank checkmate, attacking your king along the back rank when you don't have an escape square or pieces with which you can block. In this case, you must move a pawn to give your king an escape route. This is called creating "luft" (German for "air").

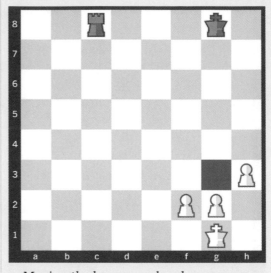

Moving the h-pawn only releases some control of g3.

When making luft, try to move a pawn at the edge of the board, as that creates the fewest weaknesses. If you move any other pawn, it will no longer guard two squares around the king.

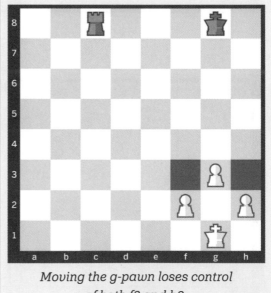

Moving the g-pawn loses control of both f3 and h3.

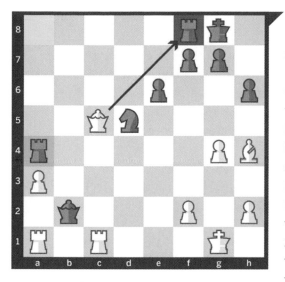

Note that making luft doesn't always solve back-rank issues. In the game to the left, GM Vladislav Artemiev thought he was safe from back-rank checkmate because he played h6, so he next played 24 . . . Ra4?? GM Shakhriyar Mamedyarov responded with the excellent decoy 25. Qxf8+. White lures the black king away from the luft on h6 by capturing the rook and offering the queen as a decoy sacrifice. If black doesn't take the queen, white has just won a rook for free.

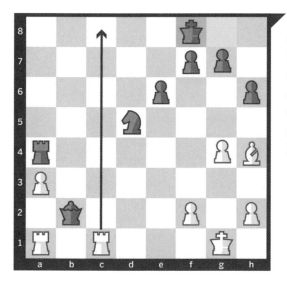

And after Artemiev captured the queen with 25 . . . Kxf8, Mamedyarov simply played 26. Rc8#! Artemiev's king couldn't escape the back rank because Mamedyarov's bishop covered e7.

TAKE ADVANTAGE OF THE TWO BISHOPS

Having two bishops is better than having one knight and one bishop, because two bishops can control a lot more squares. When the bishop pair works together on adjacent diagonals, they are called Horwitz bishops, after the chess author Bernhard Horwitz. Together, they control a lot of the board, so aim for Horowitz bishops whenever possible.

GM Irina Krush is notorious for her attacks with two bishops. In her game against GM Antoaneta Stefanova here, Krush shows their potential. Stefanova is already lost, but she plays . . . h6 (luft!) to prevent an immediate back-rank mate. Krush plays Re8+ anyway, and then after . . . Rxe8 and queen takes back, the king must run to h7.

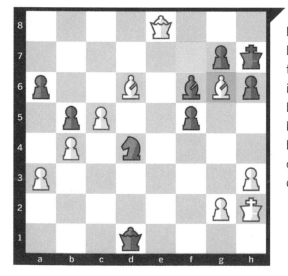

Now the light-squared bishop shows its strength by playing Bg8+ forcing the king back to h8. Bf7+ is a discovered check by the queen, and the king has to go back to h7. Finally the bishop comes around to g6 to deliver mate.

BRING YOUR ROOKS TO OPEN FILES

Rooks love an open board. An open file has no pawns, so it's the rooks' opportunity to make a grand appearance!

Paul Morphy was the first unofficial World Chess Champion. In his 1858 game against Duke Karl II and Count Isouard de Vauvenargues in Paris, notice how the black rook is absolutely pinned by Morphy's bishop on b5. He added pressure to the pinned piece by placing his rook on the open file: Rd1. Morphy checkmated his opponents soon after this move.

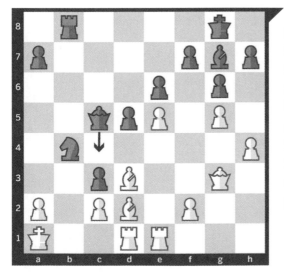

In the 1957 game shown here, GM Tigran Petrosian wins with black by sacrificing his queen as a decoy on c4! If the knight moves, the rook guards the entire b-file. If the bishop doesn't take, the black queen will capture on a2, and game over.

If the bishop takes, it will no longer guard the pawn on c2, allowing the black knight to capture with checkmate.

What not to do: Don't develop your rooks to closed files blocked by pawns. You want your pieces on active squares.

Tip: If you're not sure which rook to move to an open file, ask yourself which one hasn't had a chance to play!

TRY A ROOK LIFT

In British English, a lift is an elevator. In chess, it's a way to double your rooks and activate them on a different rank. To perform a rook lift, you must move the rook up a number of ranks, then move it over to the desired file. While this isn't an immediate, forcing maneuver (it takes multiple moves), it's how you double rooks on an open file and is a great way to attack.

GM and 2021 World Champion Magnus Carlsen is a big proponent of this middle game strategy. In this game, notice he's flouted some opening principles (like castling), so now he must decide how to get his rook out of the corner.

Carlsen has just played 12. h4 in the game above. In this eighteen-move game (called a "miniature") against GM Jan-Krzysztof Duda, Carlsen then immediately attacked black's king with all his pieces. He knew black was planning to castle kingside, so he used a rook lift to play Rh3-g3 and pin the g-pawn to the king once it castled.

What not to do:
Don't perform a rook lift in the opening, as it will likely get captured. Instead, aim to castle and connect your rooks. (Connected rooks have no pieces in between them on the back rank. They protect each other and can work together.) In the middle game, you can consider a rook lift for an attack.

FORM A BATTERY

The long-range pieces—rooks, bishops, and queens—work well when they line up, because the piece behind guards the one in front. Any combination of these pieces is considered a battery when they are on the same file, rank, or diagonal (except a queen and bishop on a file or rank).

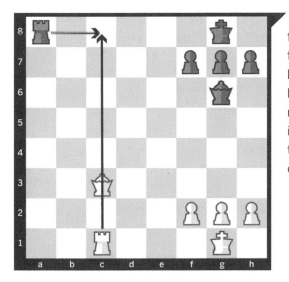

When the queen is in front of a rook, together they can threaten back-rank checkmates or helper mates (involving multiple pieces attacking the same square) to break through to a castled king.

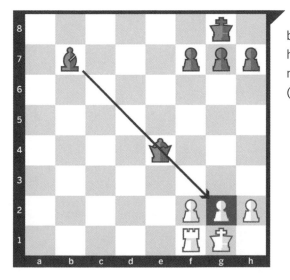

The black queen and bishop work together here. The queen will mate white on g2 (helper mate).

Additionally, when a bishop is in front of the queen, together they can attack and open a castle wall (the pawns a castled king hides behind), potentially leading to a checkmate.

Justus Williams, who became the youngest African American U.S. Chess Federation National Master (NM) ever as of 2010 at the age of 12, won the game at left with a battery. In this position, Williams has just played the brilliant bishop sacrifice 27 . . . Be3! It looks like black's knight on g3 is also hanging, but notice the bishop pins the pawn on f2 to the white king, so it can't take the knight. Instead, white will play 28. fxe3.

This game continued another 10 moves to the final battery shown here. White loses the queen after 38 . . . Rxh3+ because following 39. Qxh3 Rd2+, 40. Kg3 Rd3+ skewers the king to the queen!

White resigned on move 39, seeing this skewer and queen loss coming.

Create a battery that aims at a target, and make sure you have open lines for your long-range pieces to attack your opponent's weak squares.

"DON'T TRADE UNLESS IT'S FORCED OR FANTASTIC"

This phrase was coined by Maurice Ashley, the first African American Grandmaster and an excellent commentator. In general, you should try to trade pieces when you are ahead in material, but otherwise, don't go through with an exchange unless you have to or it improves your position.

Try not to trade a bishop for a knight unless the position is so closed that the knight has an advantage (because it can jump over pieces). In open positions, bishops tend to be stronger due to their long-range capabilities.

Try to trade queens if you are about to be checkmated or are under attack ("forced"). A king that is under attack will be much safer without the opposing queen around. By the same logic, if you are the one attacking, do not trade queens! You'll need your queen to help deliver checkmate.

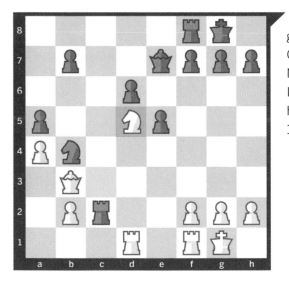

In this 2004 blitz game between Woman Grandmaster (WGM) Natalia Pogonina and GM Irina Krush, Pogonina has just blundered with 19. Nd5?.

Krush, with black, plays 19 . . . Qe6, pinning the knight to the queen (and forgoing taking the knight). After 20. h4, Krush plays . . . Rc5, putting more pressure on the pinned piece. Again, Krush does not immediately trade on d5 because the white knight is defended twice and therefore she'd lose material. After . . . Rc5, there are three black attackers, and Pogonina resigns, about to lose a piece and then the game.

What not to do: Don't trade your active pieces for your opponent's passive ones by capturing automatically. Instead, visualize the position after the trade, and if your position will be better, the trade is warranted.

PLAY FORCING MOVES

One of the most important strategies in chess is taking initiative by playing forcing moves: specifically checks, threats, and captures (CTC). Checks are the most forcing moves because it is illegal to stay in check; your opponent must spend time escaping from danger.

To better understand forcing moves, let's look at this incredible checkmate by U.S. junior phenom GM Awonder Liang against IM Gunay Mammadzada. This type of checkmate is called a "smothered mate." Black's king is suffocated by its own pieces and cannot move anything. How did white force this to happen? Let's go back a few moves . . .

Mammadzada has just played 34 . . . a5 to give herself luft. But now Liang plays the interesting 35. Nc8, which threatens Qa6+ followed by Qxa7# (note that the black rook on b7 cannot capture on a7 because it is pinned by the bishop on g2).

Black tries to hold on by guarding a7 with the bishop.

Liang plays 36. Qa6+ anyway! If black blocks with the queen, the knight will capture it, and there will be a mate on b7 next. So, Mammadzada blocks with the bishop, but Liang doesn't take it, instead playing the stunning 37. Nb6# we saw on the previous page.

Always look for forcing moves to give yourself a competitive advantage. However, don't make checks just because they look pretty—make sure they force a position in your favor.

LAUNCH COUNTERATTACKS

Counterattacks are key to playing strategic chess and are especially helpful if you're losing. Rather than waiting to get crushed, see if there is a way you can create problems for your opponent. That said, be sure that all your counterattacks have clear targets, the power of which is demonstrated in the 2011 game below between GM Leinier Domínguez Pérez and GM Judit Polgár.

Notice how black's knight on e5 is pinned by white's bishop at f4. Funnily enough, Polgár moves it anyway! She captures on f3, counterattacking white's queen.

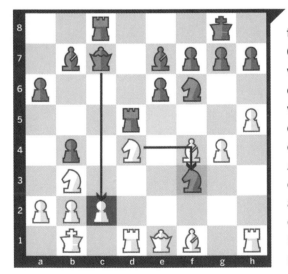

If the white knight takes on f3, black plays Qxf2+, forcing Ka1, after which black can take on d1 with the rook. The white queen is the only defender so she captures on d1, but then . . . Qxd1+. After white blocks on c1, the rook and queen attack that square, and only one piece guards it. It will be a back rank mate on c1.

Instead of the scenario from the previous page, Domínguez tries to save the queen with 20. Qg3, but now Polgár has the fork ... e5. White can't take the pawn because of the weakness on the back rank (the bishop on f4 is needed to jump back to c1 to block potential back-rank mates).

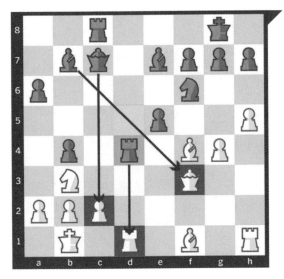

White can't play Qxf3, either, because ... Rxd4 creates too many threats.

Polgár won soon thereafter. Notice that counterattacks use forcing moves (checks, threats, and captures).

What not to do: Don't counterattack without calculating carefully!

PLAY FANTASY CHESS, OR HOW TO MAKE A PLAN

To help my students figure out where to attack, especially if a weakness around the king is palpable, I'll say, "Fantasy chess! If you could pick up your queen and place it anywhere, what square would you drop it on?" You can usually spot the ideal situation (a checkmate is best) for your pieces. From there, you just work backward: What is the path that takes you to that position?

Check out this position from a 2021 Champions Chess Tour game between GM Jorden van Foreest and GM Wesley So. Van Foreest noticed the dark squares were weak around So's king. How could he get there?

With 12. Qd2, van Foreest held on to the knight on d4 while planning to come in to g5 or h6 with the queen.

Later, So resigned in the position shown at left. White's knight on d6 is coming to f7 with check, a fork, a discovered attack on the queen, and major threats of checkmate on h7.

When fantasizing about dropping your pieces onto the best squares, don't forget that your opponent gets to move, too! Make sure the path to your target is clear and you don't hang any pieces along the way.

DON'T FORGET THE ROLE OF PSYCHOLOGY

In addition to knowing strategic maneuvers, it's important for a chess player to understand the advantage of approaching each game with the right mindset. Let's discuss three psychological factors that can affect a player's game.

1. **Confidence.** You want to feel like you can win, or at least play well, against anyone. If you walk into a game thinking you're going to lose, guess what will happen? Overconfidence is real, too. If you respect your opponent, you won't make egregious blunders due to playing too rashly.

2. **Resilience.** Anyone starting out with a new game is bound to make mistakes—it's how you learn! But one mistake can be followed by another when a player gets flustered. The best thing to do when you make a mistake is to get up from the board or screen and change your environment. Then, sit back down with a fresh

perspective. In chess, you have to let go of the past quickly, as there are always more moves and more games to be played. With time and practice, you'll reduce your blunders.

3. **Perseverance.** In the game below, longtime U.S. Champion Frank Marshall is playing black. Both his queen and his rook on h3 are under attack, and it looks like he's going to lose one of those pieces.

Surprisingly, Marshall plays . . . Qg3, which looks ludicrous. Won't he lose all his pieces this way?

But if white plays hxg3, . . . Ne2# is mate!

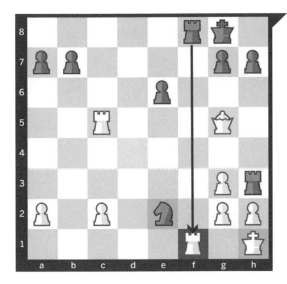

And if white plays fxg3, Marshall still plays . . . Ne2+. After Kh1 (which is forced), . . . Rxf1# is mate.

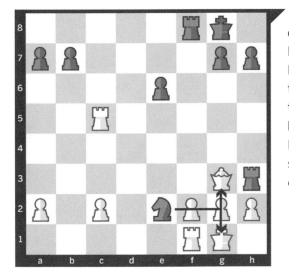

Finally, if the white queen takes on g3, . . . Ne2+ is now a fork. After Kh1, Marshall can take the white queen with the knight, forking the king and the rook on f1. Black will come out of the sequence up material, enough to win the game.

The lesson here is never to give up mentally, even in a position that looks completely lost. Keep looking for forcing moves and solutions; even if you eventually lose the game, you will have learned more than you would have by giving up.

CHAPTER FIVE

Endgame Strategies

••

In the endgame, it is imperative to know how to finish things off when you're winning and how to swindle a draw if you're losing! In this chapter, you will learn ten strategies to help end the game favorably for you. Just don't show your opponent this book until after you've won!

DANCE WITH THE QUEEN

A simple technique to force a checkmate with a king and queen versus a king is to use what I call the Queen Dance. This technique works every time, so long as you avoid stalemating your opponent or hanging your queen.

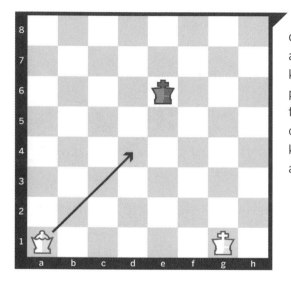

Start by getting your queen a knight's distance away from the opposing king. For example, in this position, move the queen to d4. From there, it creates a box around the king, cutting off the d-file and the fourth rank.

Next, wherever the opposing king goes, the queen follows, like a waltz. With every move, your queen makes the box around the opponent's king smaller, cutting off another file and/or rank. You will maintain a knight's distance away when you copy the king's moves exactly.

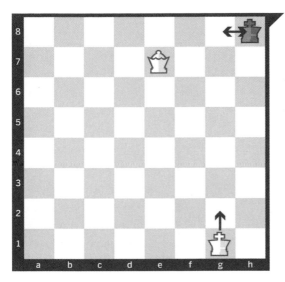

Once the opposing king is in the corner, stop! If you're not careful, you will stalemate your opponent. Instead, leave the opposing king one escape square, and bring in your king.

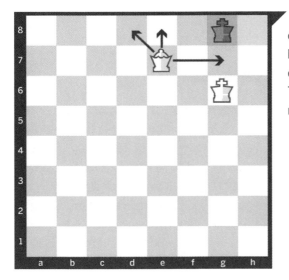

Once your king is close enough, you should be able to deliver a helper or a back-rank mate. There are three ways to make checkmate here.

What not to do: Avoid stalemates! That means even if your king must take an indirect route, do so.

SIMPLIFY

When you simplify, you trade pieces with the goal of creating a passed pawn (see page 94) that can become a queen.

Consider the material in this game between IM Carissa Yip and WGM Tatev Abrahamyan. White has a queen (9 points), and black has a bishop (3), knight (3), and pawn (1), meaning white is up by two points (as the rest of the material is identical for both sides). Therefore, white must simplify.

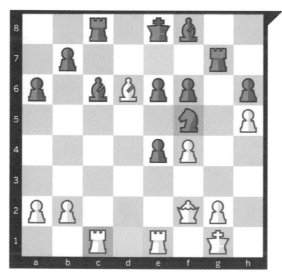

Yip plays 25. Rc1, pinning the black bishop on c6 to the rook on c8. If the bishop moves to d7, white will happily trade rooks. Abrahamyan plays 25 . . . Nf5 instead (note the knight was also pinned). What should white play?

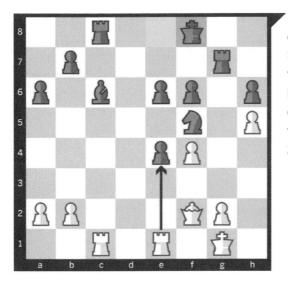

26. Bxf8 Kxf8, of course, trading bishops. Since a pinned piece, like the bishop on c6 which is pinned to the rook on c8, does not protect, white then grabs a pawn: 27. Rxe4!

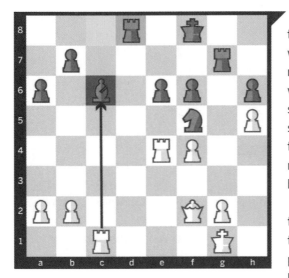

If Abrahamyan were to play . . . Bxe4, white would snatch up the rook on c8. Black doesn't want to trade rooks, so she plays Rd8. Now Yip simplifies again, giving up the exchange to eliminate more pieces from the board: 28. Rxc6!

A rook is worth more than a bishop, but with this move, white is simplifying the position and heading toward an easy endgame. After Abrahamyan captured on c6, Yip played 29. Rxe6, attacking all of black's pawns. Following a forced rook trade, white soon won.

What not to do: Don't complicate matters by going for a tricky attack if you're ahead in material. Make life easier for yourself in the endgame by removing pieces from the board.

WATCH FOR INSUFFICIENT MATING MATERIAL

Insufficient mating material is the professional way of saying "not enough pieces to make checkmate." When you're trading material in the middle and endgame, be sure to keep the following in mind so you know which pieces to keep to yield the highest chance of a win. In the following scenarios, it is assumed that your opponent has only a king and no other pieces or pawns.

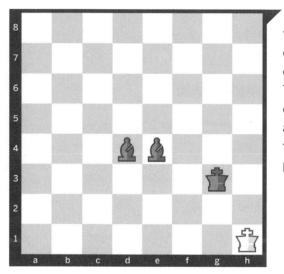

If you have a queen, two rooks, two bishops, or just one rook, you can force a checkmate. To find out how to checkmate with a king and queen alone, see the "Queen Dance" on page 78.

If you only have one bishop, one knight, or even two knights, it's going to be a draw, because no checkmate can be made. You don't need to make any additional moves; just shake hands and play again. And if there are no pieces on the board at all except for the two kings, that is definitely a draw! Kings can never attack each other.

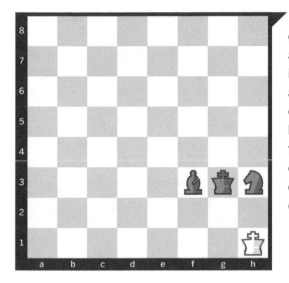

While it is possible to checkmate with a knight and bishop, it's incredibly hard, and it's quite acceptable at this level to call it a draw. You would have to checkmate in fewer than fifty moves, or else it would be a draw due to the fifty-move rule (see page 18).

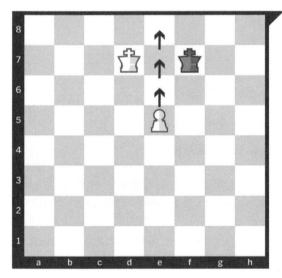

If there is a pawn on the board, it changes everything! The pawn can promote, and then you can use the Queen Dance to win. Be sure to gain the opposition if possible (see page 85), and keep your king in front of your pawn to push the other king away so that you can promote. That said, some king and pawn endgames are still drawn due to forced stalemates.

FIGHT WITH THE KING

In the opening, the king hides in his castle. But the endgame is the time for it to run across the board, attacking opposing pawns and protecting its own.

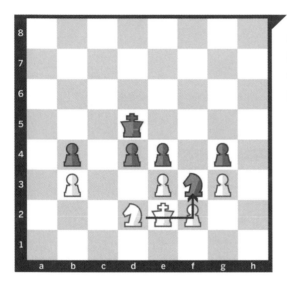

In this game between GM Haik Martirosyan and GM M. Amin Tabatabaei, white blunders by playing 58. Nxf3.

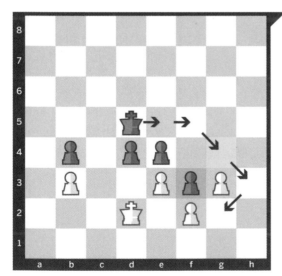

After 58 . . . gxf3+, black's king runs! Slow as it is, it outflanks (goes around) white's king and ends up capturing all of white's pawns, because the white king must stay in front of black's d-pawn to block it.

Tabatabaei can even allow white's g-pawn to run and promote, because his own queen (when he promotes a pawn) will force a queen trade. And after that, black's king dominates again, simply pushing the white king away from his pawns.

What not to do: Don't forget to use your king in the endgame. It's an attacking piece now!

GAIN THE OPPOSITION

Opposition refers to the relative position of the two kings. If there is an odd number of squares between them, the king that does *not* have to move is said to "have the opposition."

Gaining the opposition is one of the most tangible advantages in the endgame. When the kings are separated by only one square on the same file or rank, this is called direct opposition. Placing your king in front of your opponent's takes away the three squares in front of that king, restricting its movement.

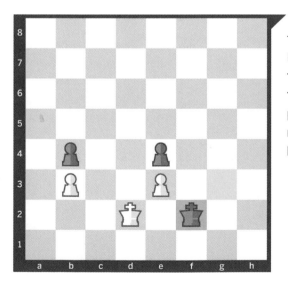

Let's jump ahead in the game on page 84. Black gains the opposition with . . . Kf2, forcing the white king to leave its pawn hanging (it cannot move to d3 due to the black pawn on e4).

You can also have long-distance opposition, diagonal opposition, or rectangular opposition, as in the diagram below. From these positions, you can force direct opposition if your opponent's king approaches yours.

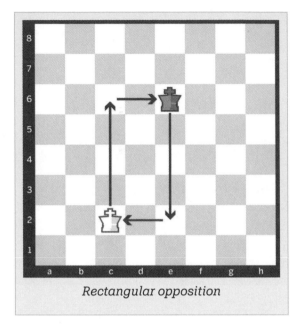

Rectangular opposition

Opposition is used to keep the other king away, both from your own pawns and from theirs. If the opposing king is pushed away, your king controls the space.

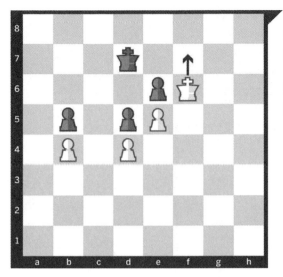

In this game, how can white push the black king away with opposition?

Kf7! And the black king must move away from its pawn on e6.

When you are learning how to win with a king and one pawn, opposition is one of the most important concepts to understand. Lead with the king, gain and maintain the opposition if possible, and shepherd the pawn up the board.

What not to do: If your opponent has the opposition, don't move your king unless you absolutely must. Try to move a pawn or another piece instead so that your opponent is forced to move their king, allowing you to gain the opposition.

PROMOTE YOUR PAWNS, PART 1

This is your goal in the endgame! It is worth sacrificing a piece if you know you will be able to promote a pawn soon after. In the position below, the white king is blocking black's g-pawn from promoting.

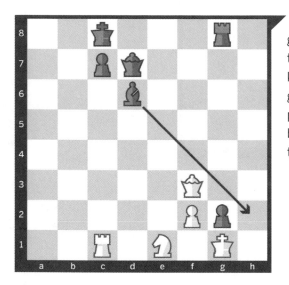

Because the pawn is guarded, all black needs to do is lure the white king away from g1 so the g-pawn can advance and promote (note that the black rook on g8 guards the promotion square).

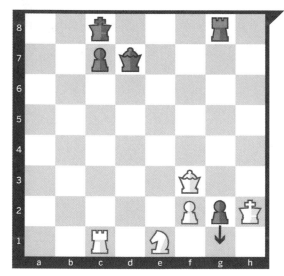

Black has a forcing check. After . . . Bh2+, the white king must capture, and black is able to promote the g-pawn (with mate!).

This exact strategy, with an almost identical decoy tactic, was used in this game between GM Ian Nepomniachtchi and GM Magnus Carlsen. Carlsen, with black, is threatening to promote his b-pawn, but the white king is blocking it.

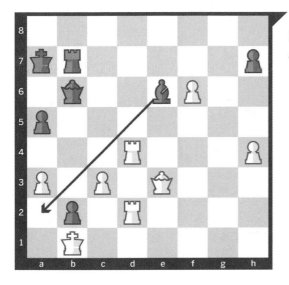

To promote, black's bishop lures the king away with . . . Ba2+.

Whether the white king takes the bishop on a2 or runs to c2, the b-pawn promotes, and . . . b1=Q is checkmate!

PROMOTE YOUR PAWNS, PART 2: UNDERPROMOTION

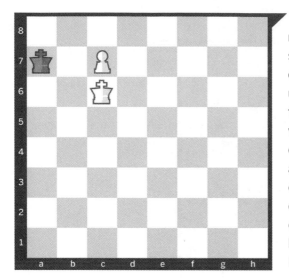

Sometimes, you'll need to promote to something other than a queen, which is called underpromotion. In this example, if white were to promote into a queen, they would create a stalemate. Instead of promoting into a queen, what's a better choice? A rook! After the black king moves to a6, Ra8 is mate.

In this incredibly tactical battle between GM Wesley So and GM Levon Aronian, So played 33. Rxf8+! and Aronian resigned. The idea is that after 33 . . . Bxf8 (forced), white has the amazing 34. Qh7+!

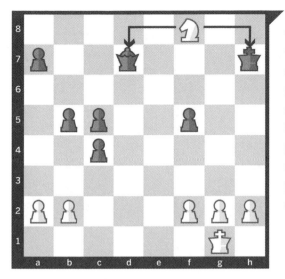

And after 34 ... Kxh7, white plays 35. exf8=N+, forking the king and queen. After the king moves, white takes the queen, and with an extra knight in this simplified position, So will gobble up black's remaining pawns and promote another one of his own.

GET YOUR ROOKS ON THE SEVENTH

A rook on the seventh rank does two things:

1. It traps the king on the back rank.

2. It attacks any opposing pawns still on their home squares.

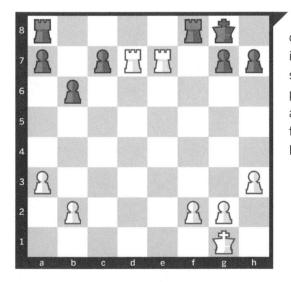

Even better than one rook on the seventh is two rooks on the seventh! Such rooks can potentially checkmate a castled king through the common Blind Swine Mate pattern.

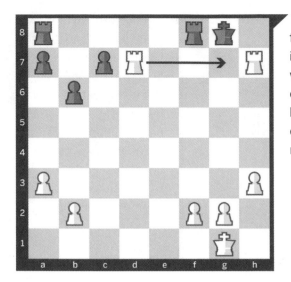

White plays Rxg7+, forcing the black king into the corner. Then, white takes on h7 with check. The king must go back to g8, and now the d-rook delivers checkmate on g7.

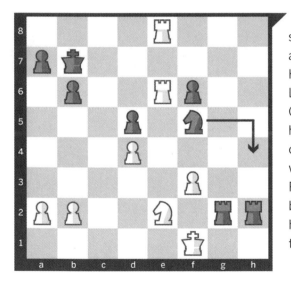

Two rooks on the seventh can also threaten a back-rank checkmate. Here, GM Kateryna Lagno has white against GM Tan Zhongyi. Black has two dominant rooks on the seventh rank. She would love to play . . . Rh1+, leading to mate, but the g2-rook would be hanging. First, bring in the knight!

After white's king ran away, Tan ended up simplifying and using her fighting king to win this endgame.

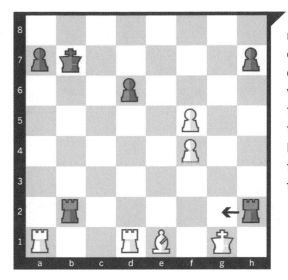

You can also use two rooks on the seventh defensively to force a draw. Black is down a whole piece in the position at left, but they have the only active rooks. Black plays . . . Rhg2+, forcing the white king to move.

If Kf1, the black rook comes right back to h2 to threaten a back-rank mate. This forces the white king to go back to g1 to defend the h1 mating square.

If Kh1, the black rook can again come right back to h2, this time with check. The white king is again forced back to g1.

In either case, black can repeat the position two more times, making it a draw by threefold repetition.

What not to do: Don't separate your rooks on inactive squares. Get them to work as a team.

PUSH PASSED PAWNS

A passed pawn is one that cannot be stopped (blocked or attacked in its path forward) by any of the opponent's pawns. In the endgame, with the right position, you can simply push passed pawns in order to promote them. But what if you don't have a passed pawn yet? You can create one by pushing a "candidate pawn," which is a pawn that runs.

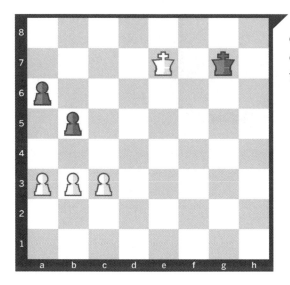

In this example, the c-pawn is the candidate, as it has no one in front of it.

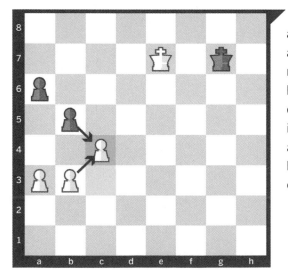

After c4, black takes and white takes back, and the c-pawn just runs all the way up the board! Of course, if black doesn't take the c-pawn, it will push and become a passed pawn. And if black plays . . . b4, white can just take it.

Check out this position between GM Fabiano Caruana and GM Levon Aronian. Caruana has a choice with his f-pawn: Does he capture on e6 or push?

That's right, push! He attacks the bishop on g7 and creates a passed pawn guarded by a rook. Aronian resigned soon after, once white's f-pawn began lingering maliciously on the seventh rank.

What not to do: Don't push a pawn that will never become a passer or that leaves your candidate behind.

ROOKS BELONG BEHIND PASSED PAWNS

Imagine a pawn traveling up the board with a rook in front of it. As the pawn gets closer to promotion, the rook loses more of its scope. Eventually, the rook will prevent the pawn from promoting because it will be in the way. But if it moves, it won't guard the pawn anymore.

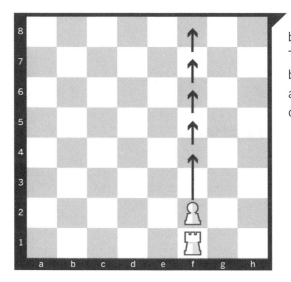

Now, imagine the rook behind the passed pawn. The pawn travels up the board with impunity, and the rook's scope only increases!

José Raúl Capablanca was the third World Champion from 1921 to 1927. He was notorious for his endgame technique. Here with the black pieces, we can see how useful his rooks are behind his pawns, compared to white's rook stuck in front of black's e-pawn.

Black's pawns appear frozen. But are they? After Capablanca's next move, the player with white, Albert Fox, resigned. Do you see why?

Capablanca can push his c-pawn. If white takes on c4, the black pawn on d4 is freed, and black now has two connected passers, both supported by rooks. White will have to give up all his pieces for those little pawns.

What not to do: Don't get your rook trapped in front of a passed pawn.

LOOK FOR TRICKY DRAWS

Never give up! Even in an endgame where all seems lost, draws are still possible. You might be able to force a stalemate, insufficient mating material, or a threefold repetition.

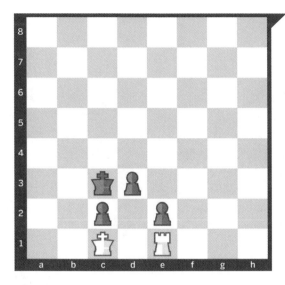

In this example, black threatens to mate with . . . d2#! Those passed pawns are super strong. What resource does white have?

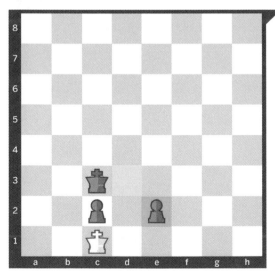

A rook sacrifice! It's the only way to save the game. After white plays Rxe2, black must capture the rook, or else white will actually be the one who eventually wins. But after . . . dxe2, it's stalemate: The white king is not in check, but it has nowhere safe to move.

Back when former World Champion GM Garry Kasparov played the supercomputer Deep Blue in a pair of matches in the 1990s, they reached in a game the position shown below and agreed to a draw. At the time, the match was hugely significant: man versus machine! (Kasparov won one match against Deep Blue in 1996, then lost another in 1997.)

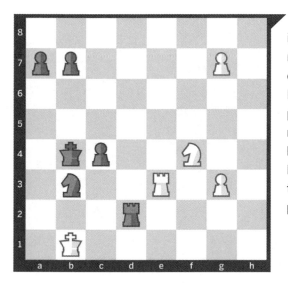

Even though white is threatening to promote the g7-pawn into a queen on its next move, Kasparov, with black, can play . . . Rd1+ first. No matter where the white king goes, black plays . . . Rd2+, forcing it back to the first rank, and the position repeats.

What not to do: Never give up! Stalemates and perpetual checks are satisfying swindles when you're losing.

PART III

Strategy Practice

In part 3, you will find 25 challenges to test your knowledge of the strategies we've covered in each stage of the game! Check your answers on pages 121 to 135. If you get one wrong, reread the challenge and its answer, as well as returning to the description of any relevant principle or tactic in chapter 2. Chess revolves around pattern recognition, so once you understand and recognize these strategies, your games will be much easier. Remember that having a good position is the precursor to the tactics that will win you the game. And have fun!

CHAPTER SIX

Challenges

....

Answer key begins on page 121.

1. Scholar's Mate

White has just played 3. Bc4. Determine the threat. What should black play to stop it?

or

2. Giuoco Piano, or Italian Game

Black has just defended their pawn with 2 . . . Nc6. White would like to play the Italian. What move comes next?

3. Fried Liver

Black has played 3 . . . Nf6, allowing white to play 4. Ng5. There is only one good move for black to stop the immediate capture of f7. What is it?

4. More Fried Liver

Black has blundered by making the natural-looking capture 5 . . . Nxd5. Do you remember "sac and attack?" What are the next two moves that white should play? Include black's first response, too.

	WHITE	BLACK
1.		
2.		

5. Sicilian Defense

White has just played 3. d4. What move must black play in response? This is the purpose behind the Sicilian's first move!

6. Queen's Gambit: QGD or QGA (Declined or Accepted)

If black captures your c-pawn on move two of the Queen's Gambit, you can win it back in different ways. What are two of those ways?

or

7. Unleash a Pawn Storm

In this game from the 2021 U.S. Chess Championship, GM Ray Robson had white against GM Jeffery Xiong. Robson made one incredible pawn move that created a mating net and restricted black's king. Which pawn move was it?

8. Play Forcing Moves

GM Magnus Carlsen and GM Alireza Firouzja reached this position in a game in 2021.

What forcing move for white made Firouzja resign here? It's the first half of mate in two.

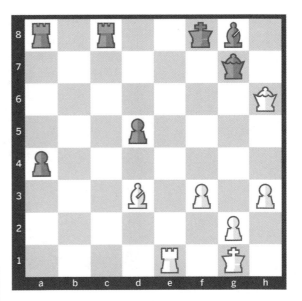

9. Don't Forget the Role of Psychology: Resilience and Perseverance

Here, GM Magnus Carlsen, with the white pieces, seems to be in a losing position against GM Anish Giri. White has a queen, but black has more material! Carlsen has just played the forcing Nh6, threatening a smothered mate with Nf7#.

Giri is forced to capture the knight and consequently open the castle wall. Now it's white to move. What are the next two moves that force a draw by repetition?

	WHITE	BLACK
1.		
2.		

10. Form a Battery

In this game from the 2020 Women's World Championship, GM Aleksandra Goryachkina faced GM Ju Wenjun.

How can Goryachkina, with white, get her queen out of the pins and create a battery?

11. More Batteries

What does GM Magnus Carlsen play here against GM Maxime Vachier-Lagrave? It's white to move and threaten checkmate with a battery.

12. Play Fantasy Chess, or How to Make a Plan

If you could pick up the white queen and drop it anywhere on the board, where would you place it in this position? The player with white is GM Adhiban Baskaran, and the player with black is GM Neuris Delgado Ramírez. First, figure out where white's queen needs to be to create checkmate. Then, write the first step of the queen's path there.

13. Build a Pawn Chain

In the FIDE Women's Grand Prix, which took place in Gibraltar in 2021, GM Zhansaya Abdumalik reached this position against GM Antoaneta Stefanova. Note white's pawn chain. What aggressive move can white make that follows the river of pawns?

14. Bring Your Rooks to Open Files

There are two open files in this position, the d-file and the b-file, and black must choose the most aggressive one. GM Alexander Donchenko has white against GM Alireza Firouzja. What should black play?

15. Take Advantage of the Two Bishops

GM Irina Krush had black in this position against GM Leonid Yudasin. Notice white's Horwitz bishops. There are four white pieces aiming at the black king, so white is poised to sacrifice. Black has just played . . . g6. What move can white play to open the castled king?

16. Make Luft

In this game, FIDE Master (FM) Tan-itoluwa Adewumi shows how every pawn move is committal and weakens the squares it leaves behind. The player with black is NM Anthony Levin.

Adewumi has played Nxh5! Look at the black pawns around the black king. They're all on light squares. White's dark-squared bishop controls the dark squares around the king.

If black were to capture on h5 and completely open up his king, what immediate check (and then mate!) would white have?

17. "Don't Trade Unless It's Forced or Fantastic"

GM Bobby Fischer, the only World Champion from the United States, was known for his amazing tactical play and positional understanding. In this game, Fischer has black against GM Robert Byrne.

There are two trades available to black: ... Bxe2 or ... Nxg2. Which is "fantastic?"

18. Get Your Rooks on the Seventh

GM Judit Polgár has black here against GM Alon Greenfeld.

Notice that powerful black rook on the seventh rank? (It's the seventh rank from black's perspective, even though the rook is on b2.) White has a slightly better position given his extra pawn, but black can create a counterattack that utilizes the rook already aiming at the weak squares around white's king. What piece should black bring in to aid this attack, and where should it move?

19. Promote Your Pawns

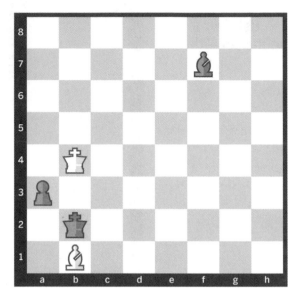

In this unbelievable endgame, GM Magnus Carlsen has black against GM Leinier Domínguez Pérez. Black wants to promote his a-pawn, but he can't push it right now because white will happily capture it on a2, leaving black with insufficient mating material. Black can't capture the bishop on b1 with his king for the same reason: White will play Kxa3, and it's an automatic draw.

What should black play instead to force white's king away (notice the kings are in opposition) or make white's bishop move?

20. Put Your Rooks Behind Passed Pawns

GM Alexandra Kosteniuk has white against WGM Natalia Pogonina. White would like to push her passed a-pawn but needs to move a rook first. Which rook moves and where?

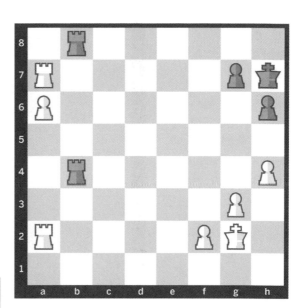

21. More Pawn Promotion

In this game, the first Women's World Champion Vera Menchik is playing black against Woman International Master (WIM) Mona Karff. Black wants to promote her e-pawn, but it's blocked by the king. What are black's next two moves to safely promote?

WHITE	BLACK
1. . . .	
2.	

22. Gain the Opposition

White to move and win! In this king-and-pawn endgame, it is critical to gain the opposition. If white doesn't, black will, resulting in a draw.

What move does white need to make to gain the opposition?

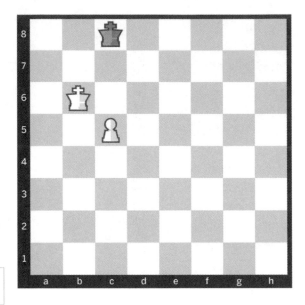

23. Fight with the King

What should GM Hou Yifan play with white in this endgame against GM Lei Tingjie?

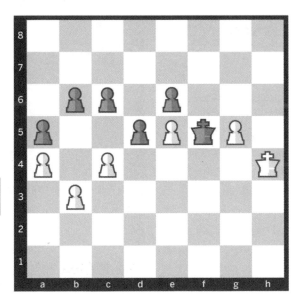

24. More Fighting with the King

In this position, the white king cannot break through to help the white pawn on g6 promote because of the black pawn on g7. What amazing sacrifice can white make to ensure the king can come forward?

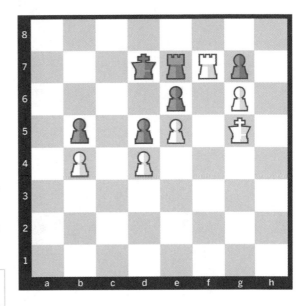

25. Look for Tricky Draws

Who is winning in this position? Black is clearly ahead in material, but it's white's turn! Remember that stalemate occurs when one side's king is not in check and nothing on that player's side can move. What move can white make to force stalemate? (Hint: It's also a fork.)

Answer Key

1. Scholar's Mate (page 104)

Answer: The threat is checkmate, with white playing Qxf7#. Black needs to play . . . g6 or . . . Qe7.

2. Giuoco Piano, or Italian Game (page 104)

Answer: Bc4.

3. Fried Liver (page 105)

Answer: . . . d5 is the only way for black to prevent white from immediately capturing on f7.

4. More Fried Liver (page 105)

Answer:

WHITE	BLACK
1. Nxf7	Kxf7
2. Qf3+	

5. Sicilian Defense (page 106)

Answer: . . . cd!
Black exchanges a
flank pawn for one of
white's center pawns.

6. Queen's Gambit: QGD or QGA (Declined or Accepted) (page 106)

Answers: White can
move the e-pawn to
e3 or e4, opening a
discovered attack on
c4 from the bishop
on f1. Or white can
play Qa4+, launching
a double attack on
the black king and the
hanging c-pawn.

7. Unleash a Pawn Storm (page 107)

Answer: d6! Look how strong that little guy is! (Did you notice white's rook on the open e-file as well?) Robson won soon after.

8. Play Forcing Moves (page 107)

Answer: Qd6+! This leads to mate immediately. Black can block with the queen, in which case white takes it: Qxe7#. Or black can run away with . . . Kf7. Then white has Qe7# anyway.

9. Don't Forget the Role of Psychology: Resilience and Perseverance (page 108)

Answer:

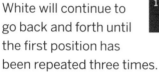

WHITE	BLACK
1. Qf6+	Rg7
2. Qf8+	Rg8

White will continue to go back and forth until the first position has been repeated three times.

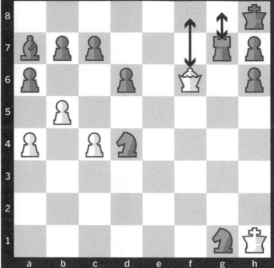

10. Form a Battery (page 109)

Answer: Qg3, sliding the white queen into a battery with the white rook. This puts additional pressure on g6, forcing the black queen to stay glued to black's g-pawn. This improves the position of the white queen: Now it is no longer in a pin and might be able to use the dark squares to attack the black king.

11. More Batteries (page 109)

Answer:
Rb7 threatens Qxg7# next!

12. Play Fantasy Chess, or How to Make a Plan (page 110)

Answer: You'd love to get your queen to h7 (via h5), which would be mate. Therefore, your first move toward that goal would be Qe2.

13. Build a Pawn Chain (page 111)

Answer: Qh5! Next, white castled and played Bg5.

14. Bring Your Rooks to Open Files (page 112)

Answer: . . . Rab8, skewering the queen to the back rank. If Firouzja is allowed to play . . . Rb1+ next, everything falls apart for white.

15. Take Advantage of the Two Bishops (page 112)

Answer: Nxg6! Do not give up the bishop pair just yet!

The point is that after . . . fxg6, white can destroy black's castle with Bxg6 next! This move threatens mate. If black doesn't capture the bishop, the white queen can take on h7 and then go to f7 with mate. And if black does capture the bishop with . . . hxg6, white can take the final pawn around the black king with her queen (Qxg6+). The black king runs to f8, but mate follows after Bg7+ Kg8, Bh6+ (discovery!) Kh8 and finally Qg7#.

If black captures white's knight on g6 with the h-pawn instead, Qh8# follows immediately.

16. Make Luft (page 113)

Answer: Qg3+, and mate on g7 will follow. In the game, black did not take the knight on h5, but the weaknesses were too great anyway, and white won convincingly.

17. "Don't Trade Unless It's Forced or Fantastic" (page 114)

Answer: . . . Nxg2 is "fantastic" because it removes a major defender of the white king.

After the white king takes back, black plays . . . d4, opening up the light-squared long diagonal, a direct route to the white king. And after . . . Bb7 and . . . Qd7, white resigned, because all of black's long-range pieces are completely activated, and black will force a mate soon on the undefended white king.

18. Get Your Rooks on the Seventh (page 115)

Answer: . . . Qb6. This move threatens . . . Qxf2, since the black rook is already aimed at that square. The black rook continued to do lots of damage in this game, and Polgár won in style by checkmating later with a pawn.

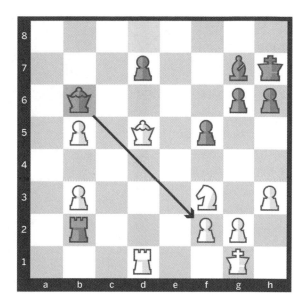

19. Promote Your Pawns (page 116)

Answer: . . . Bb3! This move puts white in what's called "zugzwang," meaning that all moves for white are bad. If white moves his king away from black's pawn (a4 is no longer available to the white king), black has time to capture the white bishop without his pawn under threat.

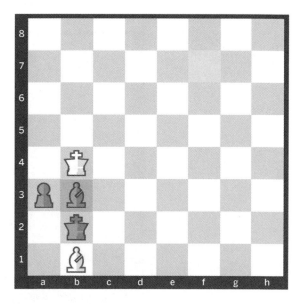

And if white moves his bishop away (a2 is not safe for the bishop), then black pushes the a-pawn and will safely promote. Another awesome endgame by Carlsen.

20. Put Your Rooks Behind Passed Pawns (page 117)

Answer: The white rook that's in front of the a-pawn should move. Rc7, Rd7, and Re7 are all fine. The point is that white should keep her rook on a2 behind the passed pawn. After black stops the a-pawn from queening with . . . Ra8, the white rook left on the a-file has all the freedom.

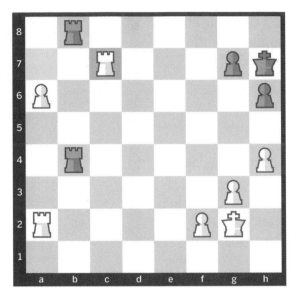

21. More Pawn Promotion (page 117)

Answer:

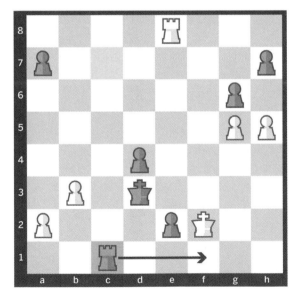

WHITE	BLACK
1 . . .	Rc1+
2. Kf2	Rf1+!

It's important for black to drive the white king all the way off before she promotes. If black promotes while the white king is nearby, white will simply snap off the new black queen, since with the king white has two attackers on the e1 square and black has only the one rook defending.

22. Gain the Opposition (page 118)

Answer: Kc6. After black's king moves to one side or the other, white's king will perform a "turning maneuver" by pushing forward diagonally in the other direction (if . . . Kb8, white plays Kd7; if . . . Kd8, white plays Kb7). From there, the white king controls the three squares leading to the pawn's promotion. Once white has promoted the pawn into a new queen, the Queen Dance strategy will force a checkmate!

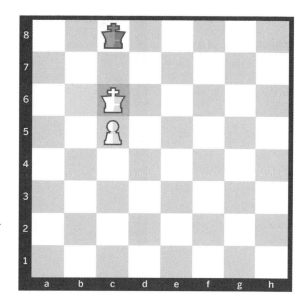

23. Fight with the King (page 118)

Answer: Kh5, and the g-pawn will march! Even if black takes the hanging pawn on e5, white can simply push the g-pawn, and the white king can escort it if necessary. (Notice Kh5 also gained the opposition for white.)

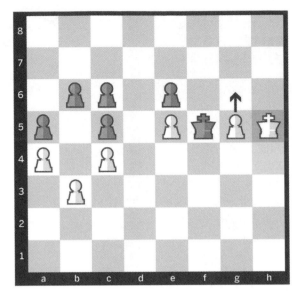

24. More Fighting with the King (page 119)

Answer: Rxg7! Black will follow with . . . Rxg7. It might look crazy to sacrifice a rook for a pawn, but it makes space for the white king to become a fighting piece.

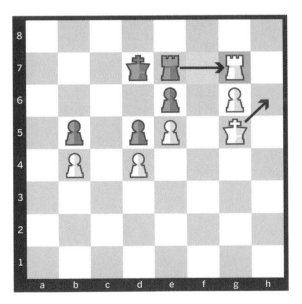

The white king can now shepherd the g-pawn to promotion, forcing black to sacrifice their rook for the new white queen. After that exchange, the white king will be in position to push the black king away from its pawns.

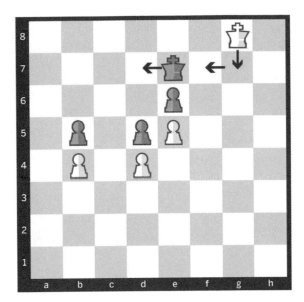

25. Look for Tricky Draws (page 119)

Answer: Qd6+!, forking the black king and queen.

Black is forced to take the white queen; otherwise, black will lose theirs! But after black takes, it's stalemate. Phew! Game over; draw.

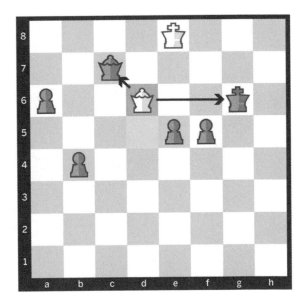

Resources

BOOKS

The following recommendations are specific to beginner/intermediate players and mostly focus on strategies throughout the game (as opposed to checkmate patterns, openings, endgame technique, or tactics).

The ABCs of Chess: Invaluable Detailed Lessons for Players at All Levels by Bruce Pandolfini

The Amateur's Mind: Turning Chess Misconceptions into Chess Mastery by Jeremy Silman

Best Lessons of a Chess Coach by Sunil Weeramantry and Ed Eusebi

Breaking Through: How the Polgar Sisters Changed the Game of Chess by Susan Polgar and Paul Truong

Chess Strategy for the Tournament Player by Lev Alburt and Sam Palatnik

Comprehensive Chess Course, Vol. 2: From Beginner to Tournament Player in 12 Lessons by Roman Pelts and Lev Alburt

From Beginner to Expert in 40 Lessons by Aleksander Kostyev, trans. Jon Speelman

Logical Chess: Move by Move: Every Move Explained by Irving Chernev

Pawn Structure Chess by Andrew Soltis

Simple Chess by Michael Stean

Understanding Chess Move by Move by John Nunn

Weapons of Chess: An Omnibus of Chess Strategy by Bruce Pandolfini

Winning Chess Strategies by Yasser Seirawan and Jeremy Silman

WEBSITES

Chess.com

Chess24.com

ChessBase.com (news)

ChessGames.com (database)

ChessKid.com

Lichess.org

USChess.org (news and member-ships for tournament play)

APPS

Chess - Play & Learn

Chess For Kids - Play & Learn

Chess King - Learn to Play

Chess Tempo: Chess tactics

CT-ART 4.0 (Chess Tactics)

Kasparovchess

Play Magnus - Train and Play Chess with Magnus

Index

ACKNOWLEDGMENTS

Thank you to Danny Rensch and Mike Klein of Chess.com and ChessKid.com for publishing so many of my articles, several of which informed this book. Love and appreciation also go to my son for understanding that "Mom has to work on her book!" Thanks to my students, whose interest in and excitement about chess generate enthusiasm all around. I'm grateful for the keen eye of editor Van Van Cleave, whose collaborative efforts allowed me creativity while keeping me concise. Finally, I'm grateful for the chess community, and I'm hopeful that this book is representative of as many great players as I could fit in it.

ABOUT THE AUTHOR

 **Jessica Era Martin** has been a chess instructor for 20 years and has coached teams in three states at the state and national championship levels. She is the former Scholastic Vice President of the North Carolina Chess Association and the founder of Over the Chessboard, an organization dedicated to promoting chess for everyone. Martin earned her MFA from Queens University of Charlotte. A scholarship was created in her name at the International School of Tucson. She is the author of *My First Chess Book*, reprinted in 2021 as *Learn to Play Chess*, and *How to Play Chess for Kids*. Martin is also a mother, poet, and avid table tennis enthusiast.